Presidio House

Paisa Slang for Brave Foreigners

Medellín / Antioquia Edition

Presidio House LLC
2026

ISBN-13: 979-8-9951420-1-0

First Edition © 2026 Presidio House LLC

Disclaimer

This book is a non-fiction educational and cultural guide to authentic colloquial Colombian Spanish. It contains real slang expressions used in everyday speech across different regions of Colombia, including informal, vulgar, strong, or regionally specific language that may be considered offensive, crude, or inappropriate in formal settings. All content is presented solely for linguistic, cultural, and educational purposes to help readers understand and communicate more naturally with native speakers.

The author and publisher do not endorse or encourage the use of profane, vulgar, or disrespectful language. Reader discretion is advised, especially for younger audiences or in professional/educational environments.

Welcome from La Vecina

¡Bienvenidos al mundo paisa, parcero! Soy la Vecina de Medellín — la que te recibe con un abrazo fuerte y un tinto recién hecho, pero también te cuenta las cosas claritas y sin enredos. Aquí el tono es más musical, más cercano, más "al cien". Tú vas a aprender a saludar como si ya fueras del barrio, a aprobar con actitud y a no dar papaya en la rumba. ¡Esto es puro flow antioqueño, ome! A meterle ficha, que la vida se vive con ganas.

English Welcome

Welcome to the Paisa World, partner! I'm your Medellín Vecina — the one who greets you with a big hug and a fresh tinto, but tells it straight, no fluff. The vibe here is more melodic, more familiar, more "all in". You're going to learn how to greet like you already belong to the neighborhood, approve with real attitude, and never give papaya at the party. This is pure Antioquian flow, ome! Let's go full send — life's too short not to live it with ganas.

How to Use This Book

Each entry is set up the same way so you can jump in fast and start sounding paisa right away:

Phrase – the exact Paisa slang expression you're going to use

Vecina – that's me breaking it down in my warm, street-smart, Medellín voice

Meaning – the clear English sense and the real vibe behind it

Example – a real-life sentence the way we actually say it in the barrio

Translation – the natural English version so you catch every bit of flavor

Go ahead and say them out loud, parcero. Paisa slang isn't just words — it's rhythm, flow, and that "al cien" attitude we love. ¡A meterle ficha, ome! You've got this.

Table of Contents

Saludos Paisas que te Hacen Sentir del Barrio

Paisa Greetings That

Make You Feel Like You Belong

(Entries 1–10)

Entry 1

¿Quiubo pues, parcero?

Vecina:

Tú sueltas este "¿quiubo pues?" y ya estás hablando como un paisa de verdad — cálido, rápido y con ese cariño de barrio que dice "vení, que aquí te tratamos como de la casa".

Meaning:

Classic Paisa greeting meaning "what's up, partner / buddy?"

Example:

¿Quiubo pues, parcero? ¿Todo al cien o qué?

Translation:

What's up, partner? Everything at 100% or what?

Entry 2

¿Qué más, pues ome?

Vecina:

El "ome" le da ese toque paisa sabroso que suena como "hermano" — tú lo usas y la gente te responde con una sonrisa porque ya te siente del mismo lado.

Meaning:

Casual Paisa greeting with "ome" flavor meaning "what's up then, man?"

Example:

¿Qué más, pues ome? ¿Listo pa' la vuelta o qué?

Translation:

What's up then, man? Ready for the plan or what?

Entry 3

¿Todo bien o qué, parce?

Vecina:

"Parce" es amigo de verdad, de esos que siempre están — tú lo dices y ya suenas como uno más del barrio, sin tener que explicar nada.

Meaning:

Friendly Paisa check-in meaning "everything good, partner?"

Example:

¿Todo bien o qué, parce? Se te ve la cara de chimba.

Translation:

Everything good or what, partner? You look awesome.

Entry 4

¿Entonces qué, mi llave?

Vecina:

"Mi llave" es confianza total, como el hermano del alma — tú lo sueltas y la gente sabe que ya eres parte del parche, listo para armar plan.

Meaning:

Close-friend greeting meaning “so what’s up, my key / trusted one?”

Example:

¿Entonces qué, mi llave? ¿Armamos parche o nos quedamos tranquilos?

Translation:

So what’s up, my trusted one? Shall we set up a hangout or stay chill?

Entry 5

¿Todo en la buena o qué?

Vecina:

“En la buena” significa sin líos ni cuentos — tú lo preguntas y ya estás checando que todo fluya sabroso, puro estilo paisa relajado.

Meaning:

Relaxed check meaning “everything good / no problems?”

Example:

¿Todo en la buena o qué, ome? La vida fluyendo sabroso.

Translation:

Everything good or what, man? Life flowing nicely.

Entry 6

¿Qué hubo, pues?

Vecina:

Ese “pues” es pura identidad paisa, le da sabor al saludo — tú lo usas y la gente te va a responder como si ya te conociera de toda la vida.

Meaning:

Signature Paisa casual greeting meaning “what’s up then?”

Example:

¿Qué hubo, pues? ¿Cómo va ese flow?

Translation:

What’s up then? How’s that flow going?

Entry 7

¿Bien o qué, mi pez?

Vecina:

"Mi pez" es amigo cercano, de los que no se separan — tú lo dices con una sonrisa y ya estás dentro del flow, puro cariño de Medellín.

Meaning:

Playful close-friend greeting meaning "all good, my fish / dude?"

Example:

¿Bien o qué, mi pez? ¿Listo pa' la rumba o qué?

Translation:

All good or what, my dude? Ready for the party or what?

Entry 8

¿Todo relajado o qué?

Vecina:

Relajado, todo tranqui, sin afán paisa — tú lo preguntas y la gente sabe que estás chequeando si la vida está fluyendo suave como debe ser.

Meaning:

Chill greeting meaning “everything relaxed / calm?”

Example:

¿Todo relajado o qué? Hoy toca gozar suave.

Translation:

Everything relaxed or what? Today we enjoy it easy.

Entry 9

¿Qué se cuenta, parcero?

Vecina:

“Parcero” siempre es gente querida, de corazón — tú lo usas y ya estás abriendo la puerta para que te cuenten lo que ha pasado, puro flow antioqueño.

Meaning:

Warm Paisa greeting meaning “what’s the word, partner?”

Example:

¿Qué se cuenta, parcero? Hace rato no nos vemos.

Translation:

What's the word, partner? Long time no see.

Entry 10

¿Todo al cien o qué?

Vecina:

"Al cien" es todo perfecto, sin falla — tú lo preguntas y ya estás chequeando si la energía está full, puro estilo paisa que va con toda.

Meaning:

Upbeat check meaning "everything at 100% / perfect?"

Example:

¿Todo al cien o qué? Vamos con toda la actitud.

Translation:

Everything at 100% or what? Let's go full attitude.

Aprobación con Actitud al Cien

Approval with Full Paisa Attitude

(Entries 11–20)

Entry 11

De una, sin mente

Vecina:

Tú dices "de una" y ya estás dentro — sin pensarlo dos veces, con toda la actitud paisa que dice "vamos pa'lante, ome".

Meaning: Right away, instantly, without hesitation

Example:

¿Vas o no? De una, sin mente, yo me le mido.

Translation:

You in or not? Right away, no overthinking — I'm down.

Entry 12

Hágale que eso es breve

Vecina:

Este es el empujoncito paisa cuando algo es rápido y fácil — tú lo sueltas y la gente te sigue porque suena práctico y con flow.

Meaning:

Do it — it's quick and easy, no big deal

Example:

Hágale que eso es breve, yo voy y vuelvo en cinco minutos.

Translation:

Just do it, it's quick — I'll be back in five minutes.

Entry 13

Eso está una chimba

Vecina:

Cuando algo te encanta de verdad, "una chimba" es la forma más paisa de decirlo — tú lo sueltas y la gente te responde con una sonrisa grande.

Meaning:

That's awesome / excellent / top-tier great

Example:

Ese parche que armaron está una chimba, pura buena vibra.

Translation:

That hangout you guys set up is awesome, pure good energy.

Entry 14

Va con toda esa vuelta

Vecina:

Esto es cuando alguien se mete de lleno sin guardar nada — tú lo dices y ya estás reconociendo que la persona va con toda la actitud antioqueña.

Meaning:

Going all in / full commitment with attitude

Example:

Va con toda esa vuelta, no se guarda nada, ese man es serio.

Translation:

He's going all in, no holding back — that guy is serious.

Entry 15

Me le mido sin miedo

Vecina:

Cuando tú dices esto, estás mostrando que no te tiembla la mano — puro valor paisa, y la gente te va a respetar por eso.

Meaning:

I'm jumping in confidently, no fear

Example:

Me le mido sin miedo, si hay que hablar, yo hablo.

Translation:

I'm stepping up without fear — if we need to talk, I'll talk.

Entry 16

Eso está melísimo

Vecina:

"Melísimo" es bien rico, bien bueno — tú lo usas y ya estás invitando a que todo el mundo lo pruebe, puro sabor de Medellín.

Meaning:

That's really nice / delicious / awesome

Example:

El plan que armaste está melísimo, vamos a gozar.

Translation:

The plan you made is really nice — we're going to have fun.

Entry 17

De una pa' lo que sea

Vecina:

Esto es disposición total, sin condiciones — tú lo sueltas y la gente sabe que contigo siempre se puede contar, pase lo que pase.

Meaning:

I'm in 100% / down for whatever, no conditions

Example:

De una pa' lo que sea, tú sabes que conmigo cuentas.

Translation:

Down for whatever — you know you can count on me.

Entry 18

Eso pinta sabroso

Vecina:

Cuando algo promete mucho, “pinta sabroso” es la forma más rica de decirlo — tú lo usas y ya estás creando expectativa buena, puro flow paisa.

Meaning:

That looks promising / tasty / really good

Example:

Ese negocio pinta sabroso, hay que meterle ficha.

Translation:

That deal looks promising — we need to put effort in.

Entry 19

Eso va fino

Vecina:

“Va fino” es cuando todo está fluyendo elegante y sin problemas — tú lo dices y la gente sabe que estás aprobando con clase antioqueña.

Meaning:

That’s going smooth / sharp / well done

Example:

El proyecto va fino, todo cuadrado y sin problemas.

Translation:

The project is going smoothly — everything organized and no issues.

Entry 20

Eso está en la jugada

Vecina:

Cuando algo ya está activo y listo, “en la jugada” es la forma paisa de decirlo — tú lo usas y ya estás dentro del parche, al cien.

Meaning:

That’s in play / on point / ready and active

Example:

El parche está en la jugada, ya hay gente llegando.

Translation:

The hangout is on — people are already showing up.

Emoción al Cien con Flow Paisa

Emotions at 100% with Real Paisa Flow

(Entries 21–30)

Entry 21

Estoy que exploto

Vecina:

When the excitement is so big it won't fit in your chest, "estoy que exploto" is the way we say it in Medellín — you drop this and everyone knows you're al cien with the news.

Meaning:

I'm about to burst / exploding with excitement

Example:

Estoy que exploto con esta noticia, ¡no lo puedo creer!

Translation:

I'm bursting with this news — I can't believe it!

Entry 22

Me tiene volando

Vecina:

When something lifts you up and you're floating on pure good energy, "me tiene volando" is the paisa way to say you're on cloud nine — you'll feel the flow the second you say it.

Meaning:

It's got me flying / super happy / on cloud nine

Example:

Esa canción me tiene volando, pura buena energía.

Translation:

That song has me flying — pure good energy.

Entry 23

Estoy en otra dimensión

Vecina:

When the moment is so good you're on a whole different level, "estoy en otra dimensión" is how we say it in the barrio — you'll sound like a true paisa the moment you drop it.

Meaning:

I'm in another dimension / on another level

Example:

Con este parche estoy en otra dimensión, qué chimba.

Translation:

With this hangout I'm on another level — so awesome.

Entry 24

Me dejó viendo estrellas

Vecina:

When something hits you so hard it leaves you seeing stars, "me dejó viendo estrellas" is the fun way we say it blew our minds — you'll use this and everyone will laugh with you.

Meaning:

That blew my mind / left me seeing stars

Example:

El gol que metió me dejó viendo estrellas, ¡qué locura!

Translation:

That goal he scored blew my mind — what a crazy moment!

Entry 25

Estoy embalado mal

Vecina:

When you're locked in deep and can't stop, "estoy embalado mal" is the paisa way to say you're fully into it — you'll sound like you're all in, al cien.

Meaning:

I'm fully locked in / deep into it

Example:

Estoy embalado mal con este proyecto, no paro ni pa' comer.

Translation:

I'm deep into this project — I don't even stop to eat.

Entry 26

Me tiene alborotado

Vecina:

When something has you buzzing and restless with excitement, "me tiene alborotado" is how we say the energy is off the charts — you'll feel the Medellín vibe the moment you say it.

Meaning:

It's got me all stirred up / excited and restless

Example:

El concierto me tiene alborotado, no puedo esperar.

Translation:

The concert has me all worked up — I can't wait.

Entry 27

Estoy prendido duro

Vecina:

When your energy is through the roof and you're ready for anything, "estoy prendido duro" is the paisa way to say you're fired up — you'll sound ready to go all night.

Meaning:

I'm fired up hard / super energized

Example:

Estoy prendido duro pa' la rumba de esta noche.

Translation:

I'm super fired up for tonight's party.

Entry 28

Me voló la cabeza feo

Vecina:

When something surprises you so hard it messes with your head, "me voló la cabeza feo" is the fun way we say it — you'll use this and everyone will want the full story.

Meaning:

That blew my mind hard

Example:

La sorpresa que me dieron me voló la cabeza feo.

Translation:

The surprise they gave me completely blew my mind.

Entry 29

Estoy en mi salsa

Vecina:

When you're right in your element and everything flows natural, "estoy en mi salsa" is the paisa way to say you're in your zone — you'll feel the rhythm the moment you say it.

Meaning:

I'm in my element / in my zone

Example:

Cuando bailo salsa estoy en mi salsa, nadie me para.

Translation:

When I dance salsa I'm in my element — no one can stop me.

Entry 30

Me tiene eléctrico

Vecina:

When the energy is buzzing through you and you never want it to end, "me tiene eléctrico" is how we say you're lit — you'll sound like a true paisa the second you drop it.

Meaning:

It's got me electric / buzzing with intensity

Example:

Esta energía me tiene eléctrico, no me quiero ir nunca.

Translation:

This energy has me buzzing — I never want to leave.

Rumba y Parche que se Prende Solo

Rumba and Parche That Lights Up All by Itself

(Entries 31–40)

Entry 31

Se armó el mierdero

Vecina:

When the crew rolls up and everything turns into beautiful chaos, "se armó el mierdero" is how we say the real party just exploded — you'll feel the Medellín energy the second you drop it.

Meaning:

Things got wild / the crazy fun chaos started

Example:

Llegaron los pelaos y se armó el mierdero, qué rico.

Translation:

The crew arrived and things got wild — so much fun.

Entry 32

Esto está prendido en candela

Vecina:

When the rumba is burning hot and nobody wants to leave, "prendido en candela" is the paisa way to say the party is on fire — you'll sound like you've been dancing all night in the barrio.

Meaning:

This is lit / on fire / burning hot party

Example:

La rumba está prendida en candela, nadie se quiere ir.

Translation:

The party is on fire — no one wants to leave.

Entry 33

Se puso sabroso esto

Vecina:

After a couple of drinks the vibe turns really good and everyone starts enjoying, "se puso sabroso esto" is how we say the night just got tasty — pure Medellín flow.

Meaning:

This got really good / enjoyable

Example:

Después del segundo trago se puso sabroso esto.

Translation:

After the second drink this got really good.

Entry 34

Esto está que arde

Vecina:

When the dance floor or the parche hits its peak, “esto está que arde” is the perfect line — you’ll sound like a true paisa the moment the heat rises.

Meaning:

This is peaking / on fire / maximum intensity

Example:

La pista está que arde, todos bailando sin parar.

Translation:

The dance floor is on fire — everyone dancing non-stop.

Entry 35

Se formó la rumba dura

Vecina:

When the real non-stop party kicks off, “se formó la rumba dura” is how we announce it in Medellín — you’ll feel the difference the second you say it.

Meaning:

The real party started / non-stop rager

Example:

Se formó la rumba dura, esto va hasta las seis de la mañana.

Translation:

The real party kicked off — this goes until 6 a.m.

Entry 36

Esto está descontrolado

Vecina:

When the fun has no rules and everyone is just enjoying, "esto está descontrolado" is the joyful way we say it's out of control — pure paisa party energy.

Meaning:

This is out of control / pure fun chaos

Example:

Con esa música esto está descontrolado, ¡qué gozo!

Translation:

With that music this is out of control — what a blast!

Entry 37

Se prendió la vuelta

Vecina:

When the vibe suddenly catches fire and nobody wants to go home, "se prendió la vuelta" is the line that tells everyone the night is alive — you'll love saying it in the barrio.

Meaning:

The vibe caught fire / party's fully on now

Example:

Llegó el DJ y se prendió la vuelta, nadie se va.

Translation:

The DJ arrived and the vibe caught fire — no one's leaving.

Entry 38

Esto está a otro nivel

Vecina:

When the party or the moment jumps to the next level, "esto está a otro nivel" is how we say it's major league now — you'll sound like you belong to the parche.

Meaning:

This is next level / major league now

Example:

Con estos pelaos esto está a otro nivel, qué chimba.

Translation:

With this crew this is next level — so awesome.

Entry 39

Aquí fue donde fue

Vecina:

When you hit the exact moment the party peaked, "aquí fue donde fue" is the perfect way to point it out — you'll be the one everyone remembers saying it.

Meaning:

That's where it all went down / peaked

Example:

Aquí fue donde fue, cuando empezó el reguetón pesado.

Translation:

That's where it all happened — when the heavy reggaetón started.

Entry 40

Esto está que no cabe un alma

Vecina:

When the place is packed to the brim with good people, "esto está que no cabe un alma" is how we say it's full — you'll feel the excitement the moment you walk in.

Meaning:

It's packed / standing room only

Example:

El bar está que no cabe un alma, pura gente buena.

Translation:

The bar is packed to the brim — full of good people.

Plata y la Vaina de las Cuentas

Money and the Whole Money Thing

(Entries 41–50)

Entry 41

Estoy en la inmunda

Vecina:

When you're completely broke and can't even afford a tinto, "estoy en la inmunda" is the funny paisa way to say you have zero pesos — you'll hear it a lot at the end of the month in Medellín.

Meaning:

I'm completely broke / dirt poor

Example:

Estoy en la inmunda, ni pa'l tinto me alcanza hoy.

Translation:

I'm flat broke — can't even afford a coffee today.

Entry 42

No tengo ni pa' un tinto

Vecina:

This is the classic line when your pockets are so empty you can't buy even the smallest coffee — you'll sound 100 % paisa the moment you say it.

Meaning:

Don't even have money for a coffee / totally broke

Example:

No tengo ni pa' un tinto, estoy pelado mal.

Translation:

Not even enough for a coffee — I'm seriously broke.

Entry 43

Quedé viendo un chispero

Vecina:

When you end up with nothing after spending everything, "quedé viendo un chispero" is the humorous paisa way to say you're left staring at empty hands.

Meaning:

Left with nothing / empty-handed

Example:

Después del paseo quedé viendo un chispero, sin un peso.

Translation:

After the trip I was left with nothing — not a single peso.

Entry 44

Estoy pelado mal

Vecina:

"Pelado mal" is when you're seriously broke and have to tighten the belt — you'll use this one and every paisa will nod because they've been there.

Meaning:

I'm flat broke / seriously broke

Example:

Estoy pelado mal, toca apretarme el cinturón este mes.

Translation:

I'm flat broke — gotta tighten the belt this month.

Entry 45

No hay con qué hacer la vuelta

Vecina:

When you literally have no money to make any moves, "no hay con qué hacer la vuelta" is the straightforward paisa way to say everything is on hold.

Meaning:

No money to make moves / can't even get around

Example:

No hay con qué hacer la vuelta, estoy seco total.

Translation:

No money to do anything — I'm completely dry.

Entry 46

Estoy sin un peso encima

Vecina:

This is the honest line when you don't have a single peso in your pocket — you'll say it and people will laugh because they know exactly how it feels in the barrio.

Meaning:

I don't have a single peso on me / zero cash

Example:

Estoy sin un peso encima, ni pa'l bus tengo.

Translation:

I don't have a single peso — not even bus fare.

Entry 47

La plata se me fue volando

Vecina:

When the money disappears faster than you expected, "la plata se me fue volando" is the perfect paisa way to say it flew away — you'll hear this one every weekend in Medellín.

Meaning:

The money disappeared super fast

Example:

La plata se me fue volando en el fin de semana, qué salado.

Translation:

The money flew away over the weekend — what bad luck.

Entry 48

Ando más seco que un desierto

Vecina:

When your wallet is bone-dry, "ando más seco que un desierto" is the funny comparison we use in the barrio — you'll get smiles every time you drop it.

Meaning:

I'm drier than the desert / bone dry, no money

Example:

Ando más seco que un desierto, no tengo ni pa'l almuerzo.

Translation:

I'm drier than the desert — don't even have money for lunch.

Entry 49

No tengo ni pa' moverme

Vecina:

This is when you can't even afford to move from where you are — you'll use it and every paisa will understand you're completely stuck.

Meaning:

Can't even afford to move / no money at all

Example:

No tengo ni pa' moverme, estoy en la inmunda total.

Translation:

Can't even afford to get around — I'm completely broke.

Entry 50

Estoy quebrado hoy

Vecina:

When you're broke just for today but tomorrow looks better, "estoy quebrado hoy" is the hopeful paisa way to say it — you'll sound real and optimistic at the same time.

Meaning:

I'm broke today / financially broken for now

Example:

Estoy quebrado hoy, pero mañana llega la plata.

Translation:

I'm broke today — but the money comes tomorrow.

Carácter Paisa de Verdad

Real Paisa Character

(Entries 51–60)

Entry 51

Ese man es una fiera

Vecina:

When someone is tough and doesn't back down, "ese man es una fiera" is how we say he's a beast in the barrio — you'll drop this and every paisa will nod because they know exactly the kind of parcero you're talking about.

Meaning:

That guy is a beast / tough as hell

Example:

Ese man es una fiera negociando, no le bajan el precio.

Translation:

That guy is a beast at negotiating — they can't lower his price.

Entry 52

No se le arruga a nadie

Vecina:

This is the highest compliment we give someone who never flinches — you say it and everyone knows the person is solid, al cien, puro carácter paisa.

Meaning:

Doesn't back down from anyone / fearless

Example:

Ese parce no se le arruga a nadie, siempre responde.

Translation:

That partner doesn't back down from anyone — always steps up.

Entry 53

Tiene calle ese man

Vecina:

When someone really knows how the world works, "tiene calle" is our way of saying he's got real street smarts — you'll sound like a true paisa when you use it.

Meaning:

That guy has street smarts / real-world experience

Example:

Tiene calle ese man, sabe cómo manejarse en cualquier lado.

Translation:

That guy has street smarts — knows how to handle himself anywhere.

Entry 54

Se para firme donde sea

Vecina:

This is when someone stands their ground no matter where they are — you say it and every paisa knows they're solid, no matter the situation.

Meaning:

Stands firm anywhere / doesn't flinch

Example:

Se para firme donde sea, no le tiembla la voz.

Translation:

He stands firm anywhere — his voice never shakes.

Entry 55

Es de los que no copia

Vecina:

When someone has their own unique style and never copies anyone, "es de los que no copia" is the perfect way to praise them — you'll use this and people will smile because it's puro flow paisa.

Meaning:

Doesn't copy others / has his own original style

Example:

Es de los que no copia, siempre tiene su flow propio.

Translation:

He's one who doesn't copy — always has his own flow.

Entry 56

No come de cuento

Vecina:

This is for the sharp ones who never fall for nonsense — you say it and everyone knows the person stays alert and doesn't get played, puro carácter antioqueño.

Meaning:

Doesn't fall for bs / stays alert

Example:

Ese no come de cuento, siempre está pilas con todo.

Translation:

He doesn't fall for nonsense — always stays sharp.

Entry 57

Tiene más mundo que muchos

Vecina:

When someone has seen and lived a lot, "tiene más mundo que muchos" is how we say they're way more experienced — you'll sound wise when you use it in the barrio.

Meaning:

Has seen more of the world / way more experienced

Example:

Tiene más mundo que muchos, sabe cómo es la cosa.

Translation:

He's seen more of the world than most — he knows how it works.

Entry 58

No le baja la mirada a nadie

Vecina:

This is pure confidence — when someone never lowers their gaze, you say this and every paisa understands they're solid and fearless.

Meaning:

Doesn't lower his gaze to anyone / confident as hell

Example:

No le baja la mirada a nadie, siempre firme.

Translation:

He doesn't lower his gaze to anyone — always solid.

Entry 59

Es de los que responde duro

Vecina:

When someone steps up strong when it matters, “es de los que responde duro” is the way we praise them — you’ll use this and people will nod with respect, puro paisa.

Meaning:

Steps up hard when needed / delivers strongly

Example:

Es de los que responde duro cuando la cosa se pone fea.

Translation:

He’s one who steps up hard when things get tough.

Entry 60

No se deja montar

Vecina:

This is for the ones who never let anyone push them around — you say it and every paisa knows they set their own boundaries with class and attitude.

Meaning:

Doesn’t let anyone push him around

Example:

Ese man no se deja montar, siempre pone los puntos.

Translation:

That guy doesn’t let anyone push him around — always sets boundaries.

Estado de Ánimo y Vibra Antioqueña

Mood and Antioquian Good Vibes

(Entries 61–70)

Entry 61

Estoy vuelto nada

Vecina:

When the day has drained every last bit of energy and you feel like nothing is left, “estoy vuelto nada” is how we say we’re completely wiped — you’ll drop this in the barrio and every paisa will nod because they’ve been there.

Meaning: I’m completely drained / turned into nothing

Example:

Después del trabajo estoy vuelto nada, necesito descansar.

Translation:

After work I’m completely drained — I need to rest.

Entry 62

Quedé hecho polvo

Vecina:

After a long rumba or a heavy week, “quedé hecho polvo” is the perfect paisa way to say you’re totally wiped out — you’ll sound real and relatable the moment you say it.

Meaning:

Left exhausted / wiped out

Example:

Después de la rumba quedé hecho polvo, no puedo ni moverme.

Translation:

After the party I was wiped out — can't even move.

Entry 63

Estoy que no doy más

Vecina:

When you've reached your absolute limit and can't go any further, "estoy que no doy más" is how we admit we're done — you'll say it and every paisa will understand without you explaining.

Meaning:

I can't go on / at my limit

Example:

Estoy que no doy más, esta semana fue muy pesada.

Translation:

I can't go on — this week was too heavy.

Entry 64

Me dejó fundido

Vecina:

When something leaves you with zero battery, "me dejó fundido" is the way we say we're burnt out — you'll use this and your parcero will offer you a tinto to recharge.

Meaning:

Left me burnt out / no battery left

Example:

El viaje me dejó fundido, necesito dormir dos días.

Translation:

The trip left me burnt out — I need to sleep for two days.

Entry 65

Estoy en la mala dura

Vecina:

When everything seems to go wrong in one day, "estoy en la mala dura" is how we describe a really rough streak — you'll say it and people will laugh because they know the feeling.

Meaning:

Having a really rough day / bad streak

Example:

Hoy estoy en la mala dura, todo me sale al revés.

Translation:

Today I'm having a really rough time — everything's going wrong.

Entry 66

Ando vuelto mierda

Vecina:

When things have gone completely sideways and you feel like crap, "ando vuelto mierda" is the raw paisa way to say it — you'll use this and your friends will know exactly how to cheer you up.

Meaning:

Everything went wrong / feeling like crap

Example:

Ando vuelto mierda después de esa discusión.

Translation:

I'm feeling like crap after that argument.

Entry 67

Estoy tranquilo hoy

Vecina:

When your body and mind finally line up and everything feels calm, "estoy tranquilo hoy" is the peaceful way we say it — you'll drop this and people will smile because it's a good day in Medellín.

Meaning:

Calm today / body and mind aligned

Example:

Hoy estoy tranquilo, todo fluye sin afán.

Translation:

Today I'm calm — everything flowing without rush.

Entry 68

Todo va en calma

Vecina:

When there's no drama and life is flowing smoothly inside, "todo va en calma" is how we describe that inner peace — you'll say it and everyone will feel the good vibra antioqueña.

Meaning:

Everything going calmly / inner peace

Example:

Todo va en calma, no hay drama por aquí.

Translation:

Everything's calm — no drama around here.

Entry 69

Estoy relajado

Vecina:

When you're truly relaxed and the day feels easy, "estoy relajado" is the simple way we say it — you'll use this while sitting with a tinto in the plaza and people will know you're in a good place.

Meaning:

I'm relaxed / like still water

Example:

Estoy relajado, tomando un tinto en la plaza.

Translation:

I'm relaxed — having a coffee in the plaza.

Entry 70

Todo fluye bonito

Vecina:

When life is moving nicely with good company and no obstacles, "todo fluye bonito" is the sweetest way we describe it — you'll say it and every paisa will agree that today feels right.

Meaning:

Everything flows nicely / smoothly

Example:

Con buena compañía todo fluye bonito, qué rico.

Translation:

With good company everything flows nicely — so nice.

Cultura Antioqueña con Sabor de Montaña

Antioquian Culture with Mountain Flavor

(Entries 71–80)

Entry 71

Aquí todo es con sabor

Vecina:

Aquí en Antioquia todo viene con sabor — hasta la calma tiene ese swing musical que nos caracteriza. Tú lo sientes en cada tinto y en cada conversación del barrio.

Meaning:

Everything here has flavor / even calm has swing

Example:

Aquí todo es con sabor, hasta un café sabe diferente.

Translation:

Everything here has flavor — even a coffee tastes different.

Entry 72

Aquí la vida es tranquila

Vecina:

Aquí la vida es tranquila pero nunca aburrida — tiene ese flow paisa que va con ganas, como cuando la montaña te abraza y el día fluye suave.

Meaning:

Life here is peaceful / but alive

Example:

Aquí la vida es tranquila, pero nunca aburrida.

Translation:

Life here is peaceful — but never boring.

Entry 73

Esto es pura alegría

Vecina:

Esto es pura alegría, de la que se siente en el pecho sin necesidad de gritar — tú la vives en Medellín y entiendes por qué los paisas sonreímos con el alma.

Meaning:

This is pure joy / steady and unflashy

Example:

Este barrio es pura alegría, siempre hay música.

Translation:

This neighborhood is pure joy — there's always music.

Entry 74

Aquí la gente es querida

Vecina:

Aquí la gente es querida de verdad, esa es la base de todo — tú lo ves cuando un vecino te ayuda sin que le pidas, puro corazón antioqueño.

Meaning:

Here people are beloved / that holds everything together

Example:

Aquí la gente es querida, todos se ayudan.

Translation:

Here people are loved — everyone helps each other.

Entry 75

Esto es de pura sabrosura

Vecina:

Esto es de pura sabrosura, no solo la comida sino la forma de vivir — tú lo pruebas en cada bandeja paisa y entiendes por qué decimos que la vida se goza con sabor.

Meaning:

Pure tastiness / flavorful way of life

Example:

La comida colombiana es de pura sabrosura, ¿no?

Translation:

Colombian food is pure deliciousness, right?

Entry 76

Aquí todo se goza

Vecina:

Aquí todo se goza, hasta un día de lluvia en la montaña — tú lo sientes y empiezas a vivir como paisa, con ganas y sin afán.

Meaning:

Everything is enjoyed here / even the simple things

Example:

Aquí todo se goza, hasta un día de lluvia.

Translation:

Here everything is enjoyed — even a rainy day.

Entry 77

Esto es ritmo y corazón

Vecina:

Esto es ritmo y corazón, lo que nos define a los paisas — tú lo sientes en cada canción que suena en el barrio y en cada abrazo que damos.

Meaning:

Rhythm and heart / that defines a lot here

Example:

Colombia es ritmo y corazón, pura pasión.

Translation:

Colombia is rhythm and heart — pure passion.

Entry 78

Aquí todo tiene su tumbao

Vecina:

Aquí todo tiene su tumbao, hasta caminar por las calles de Medellín — tú lo coges rápido y ya caminas con ese flow paisa que no se aprende en libros.

Meaning:

Everything has its tumbao / rhythmic swagger

Example:

Aquí todo tiene su tumbao, hasta caminar.

Translation:

Everything here has swagger — even walking.

Entry 79

Esto es vida sabrosa

Vecina:

Esto es vida sabrosa, no perfecta pero bien vivida — tú la pruebas en Antioquia y entiendes por qué decimos que la montaña nos enseña a gozar lo que tenemos.

Meaning:

Tasty life / well-lived even if not perfect

Example:

Esto es vida sabrosa, con sus altos y bajos.

Translation:

This is a tasty life — with its ups and downs.

Entry 80

Aquí todo se vive bonito

Vecina:

Aquí todo se vive bonito, con cariño y sabor de montaña — tú lo sientes y ya no quieres irte igual que llegaste, parce.

Meaning:

Everything is lived beautifully / understood here

Example:

Aquí todo se vive bonito, con cariño y sabor.

Translation:

Here everything is lived beautifully — with love and flavor.

Representative Glossary

(CS-02 Paisa Edition)

Parce
Vecina: Our favorite word for a true friend or partner — you call someone “parce” and you’re already part of the crew, puro cariño de barrio.
Meaning: Buddy / partner

Ome
Vecina: The classic paisa way to say “man” or “dude” with rhythm and warmth — you add “ome” and everything sounds more Medellín.
Meaning: Man / dude (warm Paisa expression)

Chimba
Vecina: The word every paisa uses when something is straight-up awesome — you’ll catch yourself saying “qué chimba” after your first real Medellín experience.
Meaning: Awesome / great

Al cien
Vecina: When something is at 100%, perfect, full energy — “al cien” is how we say we’re going all in, puro flow paisa.
Meaning: At 100% / perfect / full energy

Parche
Vecina: A group of friends or the plan itself — "armar un parche" is one of the most important things we do in life.
Meaning: Hangout / crew / plan with friends

De una pues
Vecina: Our fast, confident way of saying "right away" or "I'm in" — you say it with attitude and you're already committed, al cien.
Meaning: Right away / I'm in

Pila
Vecina: Sharp, alert, on point — being "pila" is highly valued here because in Medellín you have to stay awake to keep up with the flow.
Meaning: Sharp / alert

Bacano
Vecina: Cool, great, nice — the relaxed paisa way to say something or someone is genuinely good. You'll hear it all day in the streets of Antioquia.
Meaning: Cool / great

Rumba
Vecina: Party — for us paisas a rumba is never just a party, it's an event full of music, flow, and good energy.
Meaning: Party

Meterle ficha
Vecina: To put in effort and go all in — “meterle ficha” is how we say let’s work hard and make it happen, puro espíritu antioqueño.
Meaning: Put in effort / go all in / hustle

Discover the Collection

La Vecina Says

The 8-Volume Series

Here's the full collection so you can keep exploring every corner of Colombia:

CS-01 – Colombian Slang for Brave Foreigners

CS-02 – Paisa Slang for Brave Foreigners

CS-03 – Rolo Slang for Brave Foreigners

CS-04 – Caleño Slang for Brave Foreigners

CS-05 – Cafetero Slang for Brave Foreigners

CS-06 – Costeño Slang for Brave Foreigners

CS-07 – Santandereano & Boyacense Slang for Brave Foreigners

CS-08 – Pacific Coast Slang for Brave Foreigners

Acknowledgements

Vecina:

Gracias de corazón a todos los colombianos que mantienen vivo este idioma tan vivo y sabroso. Sin ustedes, nada de esto tendría sabor. Y a ti, valiente lector, gracias por atreverte a aprender con nosotros. ¡Nos vemos en la próxima vuelta!

www.ingramcontent.com/pod-product-compliance
Lightning Source LLC
LaVergne TN
LVHW011051110826
845149LV00015B/3457
9798995142010